MY WRITING DAY

by

David A. Adler

photographs by

Nina Crews

Richard C. Owen Publishers, Inc.
Katonah, New York

Meet the Author titles

Verna Aardema *A Bookworm Who Hatched*
David A. Adler *My Writing Day*
Frank Asch *One Man Show*
Joseph Bruchac *Seeing the Circle*
Eve Bunting *Once Upon a Time*
Lynne Cherry *Making a Difference in the World*
Lois Ehlert *Under My Nose*
Jean Fritz *Surprising Myself*
Paul Goble *Hau Kola Hello Friend*
Ruth Heller *Fine Lines*
Lee Bennett Hopkins *The Writing Bug*
James Howe *Playing with Words*
Johanna Hurwitz *A Dream Come True*

Karla Kuskin *Thoughts, Pictures, and Words*
Thomas Locker *The Man Who Paints Nature*
Jonathan London *Tell Me a Story*
George Ella Lyon *A Wordful Child*
Margaret Mahy *My Mysterious World*
Rafe Martin *A Storyteller's Story*
Patricia McKissack *Can You Imagine?*
Patricia Polacco *Firetalking*
Laurence Pringle *Nature! Wild and Wonderful*
Cynthia Rylant *Best Wishes*
Seymour Simon *From Paper Airplanes to Outer Space*
Jean Van Leeuwen *Growing Ideas*
Jane Yolen *A Letter from Phoenix Farm*

Text copyright © 1999 by David A. Adler
Photographs copyright © 1999 by Nina Crews

Richard C. Owen Publishers, Inc.
PO Box 585
Katonah, New York 10536

Library of Congress Cataloging–in–Publication Data

Adler, David A.
    My writing day / by David A. Adler ; photographs by Nina Crews.
    p. cm. — (Meet the author)
    Summary: The author of many works of both fiction and non-fiction describes his life, his daily
        activities, and his creative process, showing how all are intertwined.
    ISBN 1-57274-326-3 (hardcover)
    1. Adler, David A. — Authorship Juvenile literature.
2. Authors, American — 20th century Biography Juvenile literature.
3. Children's stories — Authorship Juvenile literature.
[1. Adler, David A. , — . 2. Authors, American.]
I. Crews, Nina, ill. II. Title . III. Series: Meet the author (Katonah, N.Y.)
PS3551.D592Z47 1999
813' .54—dc21
[B]   99-11049
                                                                              CIP

Editorial, Art, and Production Director *Janice Boland*
Production Assistant *Donna Parsons*
Color separations by Leo P. Callahan Inc., Binghamton, NY

Printed in the United States of America

9   8   7   6   5   4   3   2

I'm the second oldest of six children,
four boys and two girls.

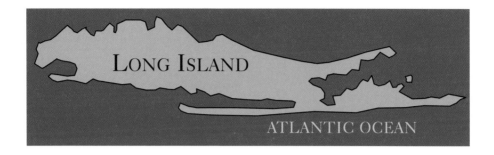

LONG ISLAND

ATLANTIC OCEAN

We grew up on Long Island, New York
in a large, old, white house filled with books.

Every Friday night after dinner, we sat in the living room,
on chairs, couches, and the floor, and read.

When my grandmother visited she read me bedtime stories
by Thornton W. Burgess. I still have them and other favorite
books from my childhood.

When I was older, I told my youngest sister Susan
stories that I made up.
Her favorite was about a girl who planted flowers in her shoes.
My parents thought that I might become a businessman
when I grew up because whenever my brothers and I
went snow shoveling, I was the one who asked the neighbors
if they wanted their walks cleaned.
If they did, I negotiated the price.
My parents also thought I might become a lawyer
because I was good with words.
I used them well in family debates and arguments.

But I dreamed of becoming a cartoonist
because I loved to paint and draw.
I still do.

As a teenager, I had many jobs.

I delivered eggs and baked goods.

I was a waiter. I led youth groups

and taught arts and crafts.

I sold my cartoons and drawings to various magazines.

I even tried writing and publishing my own local newspaper.

But the only copy I sold was to my parents.

In college I studied economics, mathematics, and education.

When I graduated I became a junior high school math teacher.

At night I studied for a graduate degree –

an MBA in marketing.

I loved teaching. My students had fun.

They weren't always aware that they were learning math,

but they were.

One Sunday morning, after I had been teaching
for a few years, my nephew Donnie came to visit.
He was two and a half years old and kept asking questions.
He didn't even wait for me to answer one question
before he asked another. When he left I was exhausted,
but I couldn't get all those questions out of my mind.
I wrote some of them in my journal. I wrote my answers, too.
That was the beginning of my very first book,
A Little at a Time.

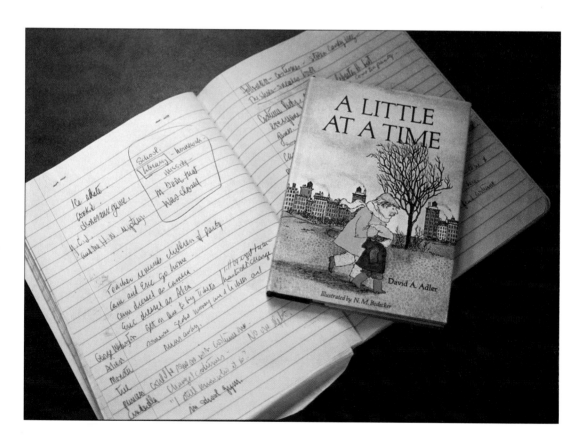

I continued to teach math and paint and draw,
but now I was a writer, too.
I wrote a few math books and a book about redwood trees.

In 1973 I married Renée Hamada, a school psychologist.
When Michael, our first son, was born
I stayed home to take care of him.
I took him for long walks in his carriage.
All those baby things — a clean diaper, wipes,
a bottle of formula, a pacifier, a rattle —
that I brought along on our walks
gave me the idea for a mystery.
A boy I once knew with a photographic memory
gave me the idea for my mystery-solving detective, Cam Jansen.

I set goals for myself – not how much I would write,
but how many hours each day I would spend writing.
While Michael napped, I wrote
Cam Jansen and the Mystery of the Stolen Diamonds.
It was the first book in a series about a ten-year-old girl
who says "click!" when she wants to remember something.

When Michael was seven, our son Eddie was born.
Five years later, our son Eitan was born.

I love being with my family and sharing their interests.
Beyond that, each has given me ideas for stories.
Their questions have sent me to the library
to research my answers.
That research and my own curiosity
have led me to write many nonfiction books.

My day begins early.
I say good-bye to Renée.

Michael and I discuss sports news.

Then I walk Eddie and Eitan to the corner.
We talk while we wait for their school bus.

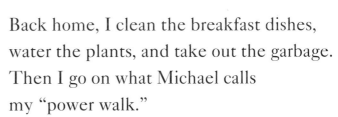

Back home, I clean the breakfast dishes, water the plants, and take out the garbage. Then I go on what Michael calls my "power walk."

At about 8:30, I sit at my desk
and begin my writing day.
My first step in writing any new book of fiction
is deciding who will be the main character –
the "star" of my story.
He or she is often based on someone I know.
Sometimes the main character is based on
two or more people.
Next, I choose the setting for the story –
where it will take place.

Then I close my eyes and think about
the character in that setting.
The story happens in my imagination.

19

Starting a new book is often hard for me.
I know that the first few lines will set the tone –
the "voice" of my story.

Whenever I get stuck I just look
at the sign I have over my desk:
DON'T THINK!
JUST WRITE!

The first draft of each of my stories
is only a beginning.

If I am in the middle of a book,
I always begin each writing day
by rereading what I have already written.

As I read, I make changes.
Sometimes I add details,
or make what I have written
easier to understand.
I add sentences, cross out some,
and move them around.
I enjoy playing with what I've written.
I enjoy rewriting.

I often work at the library.
There are many quiet places there
and lots of reference books for my research.

I write the kinds of books I like to read.

I enjoy the challenge of solving a mystery, so I write mysteries.

I love history and learning about people, so I write biographies.

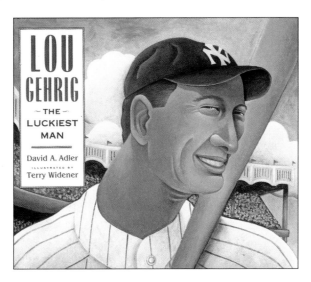

It has been fascinating for me to learn about George Washington, Abraham Lincoln, Harriet Tubman, Sojourner Truth, Helen Keller, Lou Gehrig, Martin Luther King, Jr., and Anne Frank.

I have written math, science, economics,
puzzle, and riddle books.

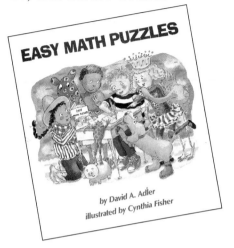

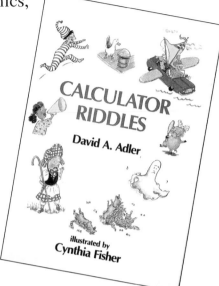

I've also written about the Holocaust.
These books, including *We Remember the Holocaust*,
One Yellow Daffodil, and *Child of the Warsaw Ghetto*,
are based on interviews with people who witnessed history.

Whenever I write about real events,
I search for quotes from people who were there.

I love to write because I am so interested
in the characters in my books of fiction
and in the subjects of my nonfiction books.
Each time I change from one kind of book to another –
from one subject to another – I feel like I am going
on a new adventure.

After I have written and rewritten my manuscript
many times, I send it to my editor.
I hope my editor will find ways for me
to improve my story. I welcome the extra work.
I want a good book.

Before the book is printed I look at the galleys –
the long sheets of the printed text – and check for errors.
I look at the artist's sketches and sometimes make suggestions.

Then I wait for the published book.
It's always exciting for me to hold a new one.

I love books! I'm so happy that I can help create them.
Becoming a writer was not a dream I had when I was young,
but now I dream of continuing to write books I love
for children who love books.

David A. Adler

Other Books by David A. Adler

A Picture Book of Anne Frank; *A Picture Book of Abraham Lincoln*;
A Picture Book of Martin Luther King, Jr.; *A Little at a Time*;
Cam Jansen and the Mystery of the Stolen Diamonds; *Calculator Riddles*;
Child of the Warsaw Ghetto; *Fraction Fun*; *Lou Gehrig: The Luckiest Man*;
One Yellow Daffodil; *Redwoods are the Tallest Trees in the World*;
Remember Betsy Floss and Other American Riddles; *The Babe and I*;
The Many Troubles of Andy Russell; *We Remember the Holocaust*;
Young Cam Jansen and the Dinosaur Game

About the Photographer

Nina Crews graduated from Yale University, where she studied art. As a child, Nina loved books and she loved to look. She grew up in a family of artists. Her parents are Ann Jonas and Donald Crews, both of whom write and illustrate children's books. As well as being a fine photographer, Nina is also an author. Her first book was *One Hot Summer Day*. Nina's other books include *I'll Catch the Moon*, *Snowball*, and *You are Here*.

Acknowledgments

Photographs on pages 4, 6, 7, 9, 12, and 14 appear courtesy of David A. Adler. *A Little at a Time* on page 10 copyright 1976 by David A. Adler. Illustrated by N. M. Bodecker. Published by Random House. *Fraction Fun* on page 11 by David A. Adler, copyright 1996. Illustration copyright 1996 by Nancy Tobin. Reprinted by permission of Holiday House Inc. Illustration on page 13 from *Cam Jansen and the Mystery of the Stolen Diamonds* by David A. Adler. Text copyright 1981. Illustration copyright 1981 by Susanna Natti. Used by permission of Viking Penguin, a division of Penguin Putnam Inc. Illustration on the top of page 25 from *Lou Gehrig: The Luckiest Man* by David A. Adler. Text copyright 1997. Illustration copyright 1997 by Terry Widener. Reprinted by permission of Harcourt Brace & Company. Illustration on the bottom of page 25, from *A Picture Book of Anne Frank* by David A. Adler. Text copyright 1993. Cover illustration copyright 1993 by Karen Ritz. Reprinted by permission of Holiday House, Inc. *Easy Math Puzzles* on page 26 by David A. Adler. Text copyright 1997. Cover illustration copyright 1997 by Cynthia Fisher. *Calculator Riddles* on page 26 by David A. Adler. Text copyright 1995. Cover illustration copyright 1995 by Cynthia Fisher. Illustration from *Child of the Warsaw Ghetto* on page 26 by David A. Adler. Text copyright 1995. Illustration copyright 1995 by Karen Ritz. Reprinted by permission of Holiday House, Inc. On page 29 *The Many Troubles of Andy Russell* by David A. Adler. Copyright 1998. Illustrated by Will Hillenbrand copyright 1998. Published by Harcourt Brace & Company.